NEXUS

poems

Ken Hada

NEXUS

Cover Image: *Eschmeyer nexus*. Wiki Commons (public domain)

Book Design: Rowan Kehn

ISBN: 979-8-9947790-0-2

Turning Plow Press

Thou desirest truth in the inward parts

—Psalm 51:6

I'm tired of hearing
There goes a well-known gun

—Bernie Taupin

Contents

Agni

What I offer
must be carried.

If I sacrifice to the Divine
do you also see it, feel it,
benefit from my
page-worn scribblings?

Any movement matters
and the journey
into self
may matter most.

Only in release,
in rituals of letting go
can meaning
be manifest.

You can't control
and be free.
You can't burn
without extinguishing.

A prince is no lizard
on a sunny rock, and a saint
refuses sanctuary
like a harbored ship.

What I carry
must be offered.

In Some Reckless Actuality

Ananke

Words are berries
on a summer tree.

Speech belies
compulsion.

Water makes
its course.

We stand
on shifting ground.

But I walk on water.

Distance

Let me love

        like a crayon
        available
        when chosen
to make a blank page
        bright.

Let me fear

        like a blade
        mowing
        as needed
to maintain a safe
        place.

Let me know

        like a mirror
        truth enough
        when consulted
to keep balance and
        live.

What She Wants

for Destrie

She wants to write an elegy
she concludes after
I tell her what that is

after she considers
grief staining like bug-kill
on a windshield

after she contemplates
new life as a poet–
recalling young love

and a fresh grave,
convincing herself
to put memory on paper

which might help her
go on–despite the tattoo
on her heart.

Edenic Surprise

Cottontails stay close
to my house, close to me,
safe from coyotes.

In proximity, they seem
almost tame, grazing
clover by the deck.

Aware of my strangeness,
they move somewhat freely.
Our shared existence

is an unspoken bond.
They have made a deal
with their unnamable fluke.

Their destiny is surrounded
by sounds of running water,
startled by electric light.

They scamper from my footsteps,
ears poised with the noise
of an engine starting.

This is their Eden.
For me, that dream
ended so long ago

I only imagine shivering hints
of innocence in the stillness
of summer sun setting.

Into Shadows

When deer move
into shadows
obscure

as cedar,
chickadees rush the feeder
one last time

and an owl
signals
his watchtower.

I move indoors,
close the curtains
and feel

removed
from the stage—
an extra

in an uncredited role,
rehearsed
and delivered

without fanfare
but true
as the part requires.

Adjusting

In shadows you slow
your pace, gear down
and brighten the lights.

Shadows demand adjustment.
Life is a negotiation
between sight and the road

you travel—no matter
how bumpy or smooth—
the danger is in the unseen

in the unforeseeable.
But this is no reason not
to make your journey

no reason to hide at home.
Be your animal-self moving
among weeds—see

what you can see
as your eyes adapt—
and your hungry heart follows hard,
and your hungry heart follows hard.

Whispers

*I like to eat my pie
before my meal
—Harry Connick Jr.*

Are you one of those too,
one of those disorderly types?

Maybe there's a society,
a fellowship of the frustrated

who walk barefoot in winter
and sing off-key

just to piss off angels
and inspire the befuddled.

What we accomplish
is nothing short of miraculous

the way we roof a house
without walls, a foundation

floating on kelp at sea.
We have been found wanting.

We are powerless, yet
just about everything holds together

and the ghosts are whispering—
ghosts are whispering.

Etymology of Autumn

We call it *Fall*
but the etymology of *Autumn*
suggests the passing
of Time.

What is the difference between
passing and falling?

Leaves fall from trees;
humans fall from Grace.

One is natural;
one results from choice
(depending on your theology,
I guess—or lack thereof).

But both speak of change.

Passing feels a bit more dignified—
the Autumnal season
moves passed us
as Earth prepares to receive
her dead.

We are dying,
and that makes us alive—and
if we are lucky (depending
on your theology, I guess—
or lack thereof) we remember
green days, and

in the afterglow of summer,
color comes to dress us
for our lonely coronation—
culling us from the herd

that decomposition—
unending, seemingly uninvited
and unintended (depending
on your theology, I guess—
or lack thereof).

The Hunter

Does he ignore his fear of death?
Maybe he faces it with conscious denial.
Shared blood evens things out.

Memories blend into one story.
Finally, the telling goes unheard.
Silence is our future.

If you hear the fired shot,
it didn't get you–
Not yet.

Red-Tail after Rain

She floats in and out,
leftover clouds
drifting away, yet close
enough to feel.

Hear the sharp pierce
of her voice—a high register
making ironic harmony
with Shirley Horn's voice
on my CD player.

Music is the blessing
of returning sun.

Song is the abandonment of self,
the soul soothed by rain.

Horn sings the romance
of human encounter.

The hawk is not so inviting,
not as suave, but she
sounds so self-assured
circling rain-dripped treetops,
occasional staccato
cuts to the heart, and I am
enchanted by fierce grace—
a tempo aching
with wildness—

and how I would dance with her
had I courage to climb,
to cling

      if only I had wings
      to follow currents
      too brave
      even for love.

Recovering

A good sun is gonna rise
and when it does, I'll receive light
and warmth and the return to health,
to purpose–and the ability to face
this mortal flight, carried on currents
I have feared, have misunderstood–
and some I understand too well.
But falling into the crazy dark–
choking in isolation–makes a scar,
a memory I will wear unhidden.
No more will I abide the terror
of an ugly dark, no more a vampire's
victim. In my hands I hold a cross
and a stake to keep me free.

Never

empties onto the sidewalk

drips
down my clutched hands
sticky like the moon

when a mother
finds her voice,
and for all we know, nothing
has always been this
circumspect

the way winter is a distant friend

the way birds clamor
in air
to discover

and then to die.

Somewhere

in Earth's sky
a meteor shines.

Don't let clouds
deceive you.

Don't let moonglow
blind you.

Somewhere a poet
stands naked

primal, before God—
pen in hand

to record the thoughts
of his Muse

to write himself
back to stardust

burning like breath—
even as tiny maggots

following what light they know
try to wing themselves

onto pages
of immortality.

But God Gives a Song

Venus through wind-bent trees
       steady, a fixed flame

              an idea of true love's passion
              that touched me long ago

only distance remains
       and afterglow

but God gives a song.

Cottonwood leaves rattle—
       northwest wind pummels
       remaining grass—

October surrenders to November.

The morning sky is clear—
       the sun is shining, but this
       is a mask worn in deception

born in the reaction of cells
       climbing and creating

a vision
       clothed in humble flesh—
       a being that pauses to feel wind
       to wonder at the Morning Star—

what is, and what could never be.

A Small Herd of Deer

In a pasture at dusk
after their leaf-ruffled trek
down an oak-filled hill,
now graze openly,

safe from coyotes,
hunter's orange at dinner.
Scavenging to find pecans
overlooked by crows,

rye grass and brown
roughage. Survivors
gathered on a stage
long rehearsed, fill

darkness like a dream,
move with slow resolve,
protected by collective
sense—in silent hunger.

Venus

The last light to shine
in the morning sky,
the last glimmer
of night hangs low
on the horizon

as if to remind us
of the spectacle
now faded, but
lingering as long
as possible

that erotic impulse
leaving, but promising
to return
and once again
shine—burn

passion's hot fire
so far away,
yet always close
to the welcoming soul
defying

even morning sun
with its clarifying trouble,
the obstacles
to bliss—a graceful
memory

of blue sensation,
reveling,
displacing doubt,
delighting in the purity
of darkness.

Sunrise

I like to watch sunrise
fill my soul
like breath

on a San Juan mountain
with no commandments save
patient endurance

where color takes me home
to pink mornings
in Pottawatomie County

where pecans
feed crows
too black to describe

luminous
like remembered guilt,
glowing like slow-built fires

flames and feathers,
faith and flight—
in a sky I can taste.

Bluebirds in December

Their blue backs
stand out–unique–
a striking relief
against empty oaks,
dull olive cedar,
amber grass bent
with the weight
of frost, the burden
of passing time.

What a surprise
they offer one
lucky enough to happen
onto them—one
also dull and weighed
down, burdened
with a season
that seems to pass
too slowly.

Feeling Winter

Sunshine and sub-freezing
temperature–frost
and wind-bursts.

Take yourself out
of the mix–be
yourself alone.

Cedar berries feed
birds and deer.
Winter reduces us.

Despite Spring's romantic gestures,
a false dream
has no essence.

When flames struggle
to light, we are
closest to truth.

December Fallout

Every year is a little harder
alone, but I'm not sure someone
would help make it easier.
Every year I trudge toward the river
I doubt I will be able to cross.

Every day is a little stickier,
briars and muck cling to my steps.
I had hoped this little hike
would fill with meaning, but it feels
like something else altogether.

Every life seems a soliloquy,
but how can I know another's life?
To generalize is an attempt to cope,
but coping is personal—my cue
to deliver lines that play me.

Commodifying Stars

The way to watch night sky
is to enter a shared economy,
to resist notions of gains
and losses, as if building
a portfolio. Instead, you should
take as little with you as possible—
maybe a hat and blanket,
a thermos of coffee if you like,
maybe binoculars, but natural
eyes are best—enter the late
dark realm, sit quietly, turn
your head skyward, let your eyes
roam the society beyond Earth,
empty of preoccupation,
of conquest—allow the bodies
above to fill you one by one—
taking only what the sky gives.
Follow each glow, trace trails
of light the way you enter
a magnificent cathedral,
or a museum the first time, or
like a child on Christmas morning
trying to suppress excitement,
waiting to be surprised—
become a gift yourself, a star
in a galaxy without rank
or class—dreaming, reflecting—
aware of what you are not,
yet what you may become—
bathing in the bend of eternity's
river as ripples of time flow
in current that cannot be counted—
free as the air, common
as clouds—new like morning
shadows through a tree.

The Music I Hear

Let these days sing
like lost birds in flight,
drawn to unseen crevices
to remain hidden
during the dark
imposed on the day.

The music I hear
feels like a dirge
drifting
among tangled vines,
dangling
in a rhythm all its own.

The Earth is too warm.
Neighbors are frosty.
Kids just be chill—
and the discord
we feel, sour notes
unclaimed

leave us little
but artificial lives—locked
in a toy plastic orchestra
requiring no talent,
even less effort—discipline
is alien

and we all want
to be native, right? We
want to belong
to a peculiar majority
that permits us to punish
any other

who gets in our way,
who refuses to yield—
anyone who dares hear

the liberating vibe,
the first notes
of humanity.

Longing

The winds of morning
sing a false song
so inelegantly played
on longstanding pipes—
an organ pumped full
of air and a player's vigor
echoed by chimes
on a rustic plot of land—
an imprecise buddha
humming precarious desire,
a failed saint moaning
a tune so altered, one
wonders if his music
was ever true.

December will soon be
gone—its diminuendo
fading to two-faced
Janus—a time renewal
will be in style, yet
regret will remind
of binding, blinding notes
that compose a life.
Let diminished sun
and arching trees house,
cathedral-like, hymns
of blustered prayer—
perplexing liturgies scored
with longing.

Loss

Never cannot be undone.
A tree falls only once.

It's more than aggravation
that accompanies the empty drive home.

It's more than you think,
this recognition in a smudged mirror
forgotten in the bottom of a trunk
packed in some closet
where only dust gathers
and a cricket or two.

I asked the wind to dance
but the cows came home first.

Maybe that's what I get for scrolling
too much YouTube.

Meanwhile

Thankfully, trouble
is usually temporary.
Though some trauma
lasts a long time, light
behind the clouds
emerges, brightens—
and if you are inclined,
do your best to see
beauty in the blending
of cloud and light.
We cannot marry
the sun and live, but
neither can we bury
ourselves in clouds.

Misplaced

I want to get beyond
the ruts that spin
my wheels uselessly
burning rubber smoke,
raising my dander—
humiliated, appalled
at my stupid weakness.

Sometimes, I use a jack
and try to dig out.
Sometimes I let my rig
sit until the sun dries
the ground, gives me
another chance at freedom—
berating myself
for the thoughtless choice
that drove me
into slippery ground

as if I can force my way
through tricky fields—
wounded and wandering,
a would-be worshipper
of a world turned inward—
splattered with mud
and grace—misplaced.

What Lies Beneath

What if I found beneath
it all, nothing but rot,
the result of ignorance,
short-sighted greed
or similar causes of decay
that now are exposed–
their true cost, the waste
of so much passed on
to someone else to pay
in a disregarded future?

Walls, roof, interior design
all depend on what lies
beneath. Any decoration
or comfort depend on hidden
truth. Unseen but known,
the subliminal belies
surface charm or apparent
strength. If I am talking
about a foundation of a house,
is something else

implied–opposing forces–
honesty and dishonesty,
the concealed and the revealed,
conscious and subconscious?
In the annals of the underground,
or in the subtext of a romantic
novel, maybe falsehood
and truth converge in some
reckless actuality–deception
is also, always true.

Something that Sounds like Mercy

Like a Breeze in Gray Dawn

The sky admits nothing.

Only the wispy exhalation
across treetops suggests life–
the appearance of darkness.

The older I get, the more I question
myself in my place:
How is any of this mine?
How is anything mine?

On good days I feel
I am a stockholder
in a shared investment
that will eventually pay off.

But what is a good day?

I think of the dying;
I think of their struggle,
the declining fight for dignity.

I wonder about tomorrow
while trying to jumpstart today.

Bits of joy, hard-won
in the fight against despair
have their charm–

       and I want to be more
       than a reptile
       that only comes to life
       in warm daylight

but wanting and being
often drift apart.

I am a boy setting his toy
sailboat free at water's edge.

I feel an uneasiness watching
my prize float away
beyond arm's reach–away–

>   It can't be recovered–
>   and I am left
>   with unanticipated
>   conflict–

the adventure I imagined–
the impulse to set happiness afloat
leaves me empty-handed, alone,
watching play disappear.

I watch until there is nothing left
to see–

>   and I am afraid
>   of what I have done,
>   afraid of myself–unsure
>   of my act–

too simple to process motive,
too stranded to believe
in what I cannot see–

>   impervious to grief
>   and the power of memory.

Imbrication

Personal anxiety–
familial unrest–
sibling rivalry,
generational misunderstanding,
white nationalism
false christianity,
select scriptures–
antichrist.

Cedar and sumac,
pecan, persimmon and oak–
native grass,
responsible oil,
aquifers and streams of water,
clean air
in a land where everyone
is equal under just law.

This is a dream
that could materialize–
it's up to us
to choose neighbors
instead of enemies–
brothers
not insurrectionists–
peace for all!

We could all
be covered in a quilt
comforting
our mortal striving.
We could be
ink spots on a canvas
too vibrant and too varied
to be erased.

Patterns

The partial moon
catches us
unaware

between
exuberance
and darkness

a space
that echoes our coming
and going

like a song
that ended
a long time ago.

We wait
like wasps in winter
in a hive

built
on the back corner
of a barn

to enter again
the engulfing air,
the daylight

warming
our wings, and the light
at night

reflects
the humming and thrumming
we know so well

a feigned freedom
so hungry
for light.

Nexus

I see dawn, and I know the story
is never going to end.
Effects are never going away
and that I must live
within the plot I did not make,
something I did and did not mean.

My contribution, a speck
of dust, like so many,
may be cornered into a useless,
wind-driven pile–
too often unaware
of any participatory benefit.

I only know that the lies
we tell ourselves–
of salvation–comforting
but false, are the very nexus
of salvation.

Is to be honest to be lost?

Sounding Hope

A plaintive trumpet cuts
a path in darkness
through weeds of obligation
to the stars–searing,
soaring, savoring its triumphant
isolation–doing its damnedest
to squelch self-loathing,
self-doubt–and maybe,
prayerfully, eradicate
the depression that knots you
into a sullen, paralyzed ball
of fear and uncertainty–unable
to act, sabotaged by the irrational
but seemingly irresistible.

Play. Play for me Maestro!
Let out the stops, force
a cleansing breath through me,
through these torturous days
when that which we love most
is bound and gagged, when
failure and loss seem destined.

Play. Play for me! Blow
that trumpet of Grace–follow
a score that, for the moment
at least, frees me–secures
me–takes us all some place
safe–wraps its melody
around us like a father tucking
his cherished daughter
into bed, adjusting the comforter
around her, leaning close
to whisper hope, kissing her
goodnight, before carefully
turning off the light.

Prayer before Dawn

Under stars, under
suspicion–maybe
overly concerned
about too much, too
little thankfulness–
but the starry sky
of a dark November
settles over me
and something within
surrenders–giving
and getting is an old
tension, unresolved–
but maybe tension
is the resolution,
maybe one season
pushes another,
the way starlight
falls on me, the way
I look up–humbled
but determined.

Change of Scenery

A different perspective late
in afternoon light, cloudless
and only domestic noise.
A young man waves from back
of his garbage truck, and I feel
the dignity of his work–his
honest wage, and the neighborhood
is cleaned for the week.
A lady sends her son to the curb
to retrieve the emptied receptacle.
His hat lowered on his eyes,
he pulls the plastic container
back to its place.

The sun is going away, lights
are lighting up and down
the street. I think of so much
that has shaped, maybe misshaped
me–only God would finally
know what a visitor feels, what
traveling unveils–probably
much the same as home–if
in fact home is a constant
in this important little journey,
this incomplete composition–
this act of being satisfyingly
unsatisfied.

Derivative

I was born in a town I've never been back to.
I was raised by a town I don't wanna go back to.
I guess I'll die in a town where I have to.

Places mark us, form our being—
the control we lack—the way life makes us
citizens with or without consent.

The way parents with undiscerning
desperation did what they thought to do—
and what they did not think to do.

I guess I too follow the current of a river
I cannot see—sometimes I paddle
as if I'm in charge—steering

in a way that seems to make sense,
but really, I wonder if the boat and the oar
are just crude conspirators.

Eudaimonia

Home is a collection
of atoms—this
essential base

fooling ourselves
into substantive
substance.

I close my eyes
and believe
the un-seeable

matters,
taking so much
for granted

even as sentience
becomes
sentimental

and what we think
we know gropes
groundward.

Song for a Friend in Summer

And the mandolin jangles on
In the shivering breeze
               —Paul Verlaine

for Gianna

With winter behind her
she lies on her favorite blanket
on the sun-warmed sands
at a beach she has known,
a place her imagination covets,
clings to like breath itself.

Yet here she is so far removed
from childhood and the place
that made her feel known, gave
her a feeling that life was a gift,
something she could never
outgrow, and God, then somewhat
unknown, was knocking on
the door of her heart—a caller
she would one day welcome
through grief. Though mis-
understanding his manner
and motive, she tuned her ear
to the divine song.

If life is a tragic opera, still
there are beautiful moments, arias
that rise and fall, graceful melodies
that consume, that consummate,
that soothe the soul even as
temperate sun on sentient flesh
in summer sand mold her.

The breezes fly about her.
Life so restless, so utterly true,
indefensible, causes her to recoil

into grace, to trust the unknown–
her own private journey,
her independent self,
her responsibility,
her joy in survival–

            her happy body
in the sun. The cool breeze
tipping the waving water
only put her more in touch
with herself–the blanket,
the shore, the music–past
and present–a future coming
hard and deliberate–nothing
can replace the little girl
who, even then, was aware
of what she could not name,
but might one day find.

Cardinal in Molt

Renewal has its price.
Surviving the loss
of color–feathers
glossy and bold, now
wrinkled and drab,
fall unnoticed,
unceremoniously,
leaving a dull image
of my former self.

A brilliance now gone,
I have no choice
but to wait, enduring
my time of humility–
trying to sing myself
strong, reminded
of what I owe–a claim
on my color, borrowed
for a season.

Crow Sonnet

Two crows stumble
through air past me—
determined wings
driving hard, eyes locked
on some treetop
where they will land
with surprising grace,
sit princely, join
fellows in raucous
exchange—like proud
members in the House
of Commons—or
newfound brothers
in a noisy bar.

Trees

after William Carlos Williams

for Phillip Carroll Morgan

They are your friends
my Chickasaw brother tells me
with a reverent tone,
and I nod
and think about that.

I think of that often
when I look at the hillside
covered with Oak,
see them stand unflinching,
stronger than sin,
bound by roots
overlooked–
a community of desire.

Sometimes I forget their struggle
to make themselves a place
of opportunity, a space to grow,
to withstand wind
to serve me.

Even beset by drought and ice,
they are everything
I wish for myself.

Am I wrong
to wish to be strong?

Am I glib, superficial
or self-serving
to dream a life consequential
and enduring?

That Which I Cannot Voice

The darkening that is not
absence of light may settle
anytime unaware–but
no longer surprising–moods
of my life return
in alternating patterns
to remind me of that
which I cannot voice.

Confusing to me,
and incomprehensible
to others, stubborn truth
stains my reflection.
Most days, I resist its pull,
outrun its push–but to ignore
this awkward ache
is to admit its presence.

The annoyance of knowing
myself, while trying
to swim against the current
is a real force–
what I think I know
fights what I know,
confronts my desire.

I supervise my silence.

Imperfect Skies

But when that which is perfect
is come, then that which is in part
shall be done away.
       —1 Corinthians 13:10

Some evenings
on the back deck
I look up into sky
to see planets and stars
filling the darkness,
and I am enthralled
to think that ancient Greeks
watched many of these
same lights fill
the universal void.

I think of beginnings—
astronomy and democracy—
however imperfect—
struggling to emerge
with human promise.
I worry we are at the end
of democracy—however
imperfect—and for a moment,
the glory in the skies
is interrupted.

But hope returns. I pray
my grandsons will know
freedoms I have enjoyed—
however imperfect—
that their skies will fill
with brightness—that something
beyond political violence
may be their destiny—
that they will know the glow
of a peaceful flame.

Betrayal

The way one day
gives way to another—
night intermediating
a pattern of losing,
a legacy of loss.

Chickadees arrive
at the empty feeder looking
for a continuing gift.
They leave unsatisfied.

Expectation,
denial,
acquiescence—

the survivor's Trinity
whose praxis keeps us

moving,
guessing,

imagining love
like a cup of coffee
so pleasingly tasted,
too soon forgotten—

fragile sublimation

on a windless morning—
crows and distant cars,
cattle in the field—
mute and unknowing.

July 1, 2024

after Quraysh Ali Lansana

There may be some hope
on the horizon–some new verse
to an old, old tune–replayed
like weather, coming and going,
rising and falling–an eternity
in motion where the ancestors
live and move and have their being.
Dying is necessary–Whitman
and Miss Emily converge
in the hearts of minor poets
who speak beyond a president's
immunity–that supreme betrayal
quashing any attempt to appeal–
except truth petitioned in the skies.

Blessed are the Poor

The dignity of sweeping
is a repetitious task.

Who are you?
What are you?

The poet at his pipe remembers
days with a broom, or
was it a claw hammer, or
a paint brush, or
a handful of weeds?

No matter.

We are our own Christ
and Golgotha may last a lifetime

especially when Republicans
play power games—when relief,
or minimum wage are sins
against the American beast.

Good Friday occurs every day,
and Resurrection Sunday seems
like story-time a circle of children
read, and are told by a kind soul
to see themselves redeemed—

which is to say—redistributed.

Of Falling

After shrimp for breakfast
I sit down to a cigar and a book–
Hemingway comes to mind.

Did he eat shrimp for breakfast?
Did he even eat, or just drink rum
to start his day?

I still don't understand how one
can be so aware of his art,
yet so oblivious.

Reading Hemingway is like fishing
dry flies in Montana–whitefish
and trout both strike

the surface bug with vigor, but one
is not beautiful, not as satisfying
as the other.

But you set the hook, play the fish
into your net and admire
its hunger.

You release the fish, shrug, withdraw
into the surroundings, breathe
and cast again.

The existential anguish we wear,
like cumbersome waders
over treacherous

slippery stone in swift water,
awkwardly protects us,
comforts us

by dutifully repelling the stream
of violence pushing—water
that never ends

never relinquishes. Even seasoned
fishermen find that routine
can be irksome.

The addiction to setting a hook
must be balanced with the solemnity
of seeking and casting

and remembering to respect
the dangers underfoot
without fearing a fall

with determination to get up
after a fall. Giving in to fear
is to die prematurely

unnaturally. Falling
is part of the game. We are not
sure-footed like bears.

We lack the fins of trout.
Ospreys above, glide like gods
while we look up

with marvel, then inward
with cautious abandonment.
My cigar is burning

as I sketch these lines.
I wonder how today might have started
with bacon and eggs?

Ambiguity

What visions I awaken to—
a black and white film
clarifying while I pour coffee
into a familiar cup—
soundless—the hero
has yet to emerge, his
conflict feels familiar.

I am beginning to see
the resolution may not
be as satisfying as I
had hoped—incomplete
theology ever at odds
with the truth of experience
lived in confusion.

The bundle of impulses
dancing like middle-school
prom driven by hormones
misunderstood, mismanaged,
an aching heart without
the words to explain—
a painted pony pounding

his hooves on a prairie
in the coming dawn, unsure
of so much except this one
certainty—parades
are for show, while freedom
finds the unbridled soul,
beckons, believes

all things, even silence,
matters—that void longing
to be filled. I wake
to roof-softened raindrops
puddling at my feet.

First light arrives
purring like a cat.

Anger

Can an angry poem be beautiful?

Can beauty remedy anything real?

Love covers a multitude of sins.

And I don't want to be a sinner—
not that kind anyway.

We are known by anger.
We are remembered.
We are misunderstood,
misrepresented—
which only fuels anger.

Would anyone say a fire
in mountain pines
has aesthetic appeal,
is lyrical?

Balance, the sages teach,
is vital—balance—
equilibrium—

going with the flow,
never sweating,
rolling with the punches,
turning the other cheek

while institutions undermine
humanity
even as weaponizing
becomes normal.

Is passive aggression normal?

The angry man consumes himself,
and this is what I fear.

But I also know combustion
is the first stage of a running engine.

Even striking a match is violent.
Friction and fraction
are related, aren't they?

Our only hope,
my only faith
is the greening hillside
so tender
in its newness

after the fire.

Detachment

I stick tight
to fabric that confronts,
that covers me.

My unanswered prayer
is thirst
unquenchable.

What apparition
do I see,
between visions

in my little forest,
my inadvertent life,
the leaves of home?

Youth celebrates
vacillating images
of self

a drama inchoate,
like a pathetic farmer
digging

his planted seeds
to assess
their growth

a forced fiction,
a novel mistaken
for redundancy.

Habits and heartbeat
both have rhythm,
but skewed

rites of passage,
cling to me,
cloud my vision

with ardent breath
so close,
but so far away.

Like Mercy

The coldness that means everything–
    a carnival unmoving, gathers
    bleakness–and you hear yourself

confessing what you have rarely said
    aloud–and the sound of your voice
    cracks like field stone frozen.

In the short, last days of December
    a bird shakes a branch
    just to live.

You look out into morning and hear
    a song buried
    deep within

trickle into melody–as memory,
    like sun poking
    through dormant timber

expands until a canvas is complete
    and you are captured by the colors
    of your exhibit.

A box has been opened and you see
    what you hoped never to see again,
    but you have always known

never returning has never been an option;
    it is a fantasy as deceitful
    as distant December sun

on the eve of January's resolution–
    when morning wind murmurs
    something that sounds like mercy.

Blurred and Ultimately Nameless

Once More, the Moon

and a broken melody
coursing tall grass

like November, hesitant
at first, then the oceanic tide.

Will the father of your lies
rise with the fall
of darkness

will your self-talk
ever wake in truth

or will you wear a brand
like an orphaned calf
waiting in line, stunned,
patient as dirt?

Reaching

I'm thinking of a grave lying alone
in a crowded cemetery filled
with private grief
beneath an elm reaching
higher than ever thought possible—
leaves, yellowing to brown,
falling on gray stubble,
falling on rusty granite,
sticky with October mist—
leaving branches bare,
empty as a coffin on sale
at the mortuary—leafless,
but for all its worth, reaching
into never-ending sky.

The Sea at Sunrise

She seems limited–framed
like a painting–with a beginning
as far as I can see,
and ending at my feet–
now gaining light
on this sandy shore–low tide
waves stirring melancholy
as if what I thought I knew
of endlessness ends–
and my presupposition
of eternity may prove untrue.

Surely only a horizon's
shadows make it seem so.
Light will soon arrive, won't it,
and change everything,
reestablish my cherished belief,
my hopeful stagger
confirmed by my sight,
by seeing what I imagine
and imagining what I see–
an eternity of self-imposed,
self-important knowing?

When light returns,
when I regain belief, refrain
from temporal accusation,
momentary uncertainty,
historical illusion,
then the painting will be a fiction
unveiled–won't it?
But what of the frame,
that indisputable parameter
again, for a time ignored
as much as doubted?

Symmetry

At 3:33am I awaken
to the myth I fell into.
It took me three nights to dig
out—my borrowed shovel
bent like half-truths barked
at a county fair.

Coffee and yellow curry—
the door of the fridge turns
and rain outside will soon float
the boat god told me to build.

At least I think it was god—
who knows when sleepy voices
send mixed signals—who
knew righteousness
and an old, old story

would melt butter while
lightning strikes a place
I will never go—who knew
the Savior's cross

would be sewn together
from scraps of an abandoned ship
decaying beach-side
after centuries of storm-driven
tides—winter

may not come again;
winter may never leave.
We have become winter
but are too pale to notice.

But the digits on my devices
all point to good luck
so my belief is confirmed—

this enshrined moment
feels like summer.

What You Hear in an Empty House

What you hear in an empty house
at 4am echoes down the hall,
arcs across a sofa and favorite chair,
settles like cigar smoke on curtains
still as stone, beside sleepy plants.

An occasional dripping faucet
sounds too loud for such a tiny drop,
too profound for its intermittence.
Even on a windless morning the house
creaks, like an old man's joints.

The fridge kicks on for a short fury
of energy, then fades into silence.
Once you settle into your chair
and satisfy yourself with the curious
harmlessness of quiet occurrences

the work of the soul may start—
the subtle way imagination and faith
coalesce with reason and doubt
to re-sharpen your will—a double-edged
blade to be handled with care.

What you hear in an empty house
at 4am is a whetstone—receiving
and giving—until the blade shines
like a mirror—and looking inward
you see yourself—and consider

the blade that cuts both ways—
that makes living and dying
like a tree that grows by dropping
seed, relinquishing, losing
but gaining rings—a record

of a life covered with bark,
cradled in a cosmos,

known only to yourself,
imagined by some—exposed
to the curious at death.

Tent Revival

Under that canvas
the Holy Ghost
spooked sin
and sanctification.

A preacher sweated,
people moaned
and guilt floated
like a moccasin on pure water.

Beyond the stakes,
dew gathered on grass,
fireflies at the edge
of pasture and timber.

An owl waiting,
whippoorwills
and a choir of coyotes
are quiet.

Amber light bulbs flicker,
a twenty-watt amp
and a scratching mic
generating

power on earth and in sky—
demons mocking though
for a time, driven
to outer dark.

With uneven meter,
hymns rose and fell
with the fervor
of a thunderstorm

holiness gurgling
like a cavernous spring hidden
hillside–unguarded
and overgrown.

False Prophet

Narrow as a coffin,
he knows nothing but impulse–
hermeneutics is a sin to him
and power is everything ordained
within the glow of circumstance,
prayed over by a perverted mother
and a mask-wearing father.

He secretly worries about everything
outside his walls–sitting
as a cross-legged novice before Fox
News–writhing in sarcasm
that would make Satan smile,
if only he could get a word
in edgewise.

The Color of Faith

A woman stands on the shoulder of my road
several days a week, dressed in white,
hat to toe, with a sign draped around her shoulders
saying that Jesus is coming
and that I must repent.

I'm sure she is moved by the idea
that the world is in terrible shape
and America must be made great again,
which is to say America must read the Bible
the way she reads it.

I guess I would be more convinced if she wore
a different color—maybe bruised purple,
or more likely, blood red.

To a Dogmatist

Sit down your ass
and let the curtain be—
the window to respectability opens
from the inside—
the lock at your command
fingers the means of grace.

The hat the stupid proud wear
lowered over eyes squinting with betrayal,
puffed like a thunderhead in July—
full of your pious self—teasing
the fields before blowing away
your promise—empty as a church pew
on Tuesday morning—you stand
like a dry fountain in a slummy park
tarnished with the shit of pigeons—
dry as dirt and too dull
to know the death that wears you.

I praise God for your obstinacy—
you give me purpose.
I am defined by opposing you.

I take my place at a Last Supper—
joining justice-seeking disciples—
fearful and uncertain—but dining
on the bread of eternity—our hunger
filled despite our poverty.

Unaware that always we will look
back on this night
with the tempered gladness
that sustains the wounded,
the humble—if not joy, at least
a respectful acceptance
of the good death we drank,
the shared suffering savored,
the breath we inhaled.

We walk away into the present—
the window wide open,
eyes fixed on forever.

Vigil at 3am.

Here I am again outside
in the deep of night–
insomnia may be an ironic gift
ushering me into the presence
of stillness, the oddity
of unfamiliar night sounds.

Tonight, the declining moon
casts an eerie shadow
across my rustic vista.

I am thinking of Melissa
and Mark Hortman,

pray their children
find strength
I can hardly imagine
in a land lost with the lust of blood.

Insomnia: January 6

Like a parent
taking the hand
of a child

we cross thresholds
of destiny

to be citizen
of a violent, oppressive nation

Or:

To be citizen
of a violent, oppressive nation

we cross thresholds
of destiny

like a parent
taking the hand
of a child

Minnesota Reign

for Renee Nicole Good

A fuzzy, half-full moon
now hidden behind low clouds
    prevents the light of dawn.
In this allegory, let rain be evil,
    thunder its warning.
Let the evil rain remain suspended
    though thunder sounds
its ominous sounds–we are
    a nation bent toward hell,
drinking the fake blood of antichrist,
    gleefully releasing little boy
fantasies of dressing up in masked
    costumes, playing with guns,
strutting with repulsive swagger,
    arrogance befitting a Supreme
Court Justice. What a cliche!
    Where is Goebbels to film it,
to glorify its self-justification, gaining
    the praise of ICE harlot Noem?
I still hear thunder, and I'm grateful;
    but hate reigns in Minneapolis.

If

I knew
or
I believed
or
helplessly felt

the stigma of indifference

wafting
like campfire smoke
beside
a river that runs
counter
to most things human

or thawing
like stubborn ice dripping
from a roof

then what?

Then the downy woodpecker
could be my confidant
and I would realize a dying elm
has purpose

and I might learn
to face the sky.

The Unknown

after Roberto Calasso

I want the unknown,
the unknowable,
the patience of grief
undisturbed
by digitalization.

Give me the analogue
where a soul is possible,
where power
is realized in humble
discovery

the irony of prayer,
the unnamable
unction that calls
like wind
across the void

like water
soothing effort
with eternal warning,
like dirt
that remains constant

this folly,
this collective
at home with birds
and mammals,
even reptiles.

I survey the past
not to change the future
but to know my free self,
limited but aware,
growing with death.

Geese at Night

They sound foreign at first,
something strange in the distance
gaining, haunting, growing louder
through un-seeable horizon
until focused, and I realize
they are itinerants
flying low in dark skies.

How uniform I have seen them
in morning light, and though
I cannot see them now,
I believe their formation
is just as true, just as purposed
to some destination
they will know when found.

This I hear, and I remember,
and because I know
this choreography,
their trumpeted cadence,
darkness loses its fear.
I join them winging
into obscurity.

October is a Sin of Omission

Fire falls like stone—
    like stone, fire
    falls all around,
    hard, soundless—
    discretion-less.

Failure to notice changes
    nothing. The end
    of everything
    is beginning.

We have not done enough
    because we have
    done too much.

A strawberry-blonde lady smiled
    at me—and she
    is no cliché

But I'm as innocuous
    as the UPS
    guy walking by—
    box in hand,
    brown shorts.

The streets peacefully roll past.
    I like the sun
    in the window.
    I like the blue
    above it all.

I like confessing—even things
    I don't do—sins
    I am afraid
    to commit.

Maybe I like October because
    I am reduced
    to sumac
    hanging red by
    a sagging fence.

I'm not accountable to Time
    am I? Am I
    responsible
    for dying

For counting down the days—
    these venial days?

When Stars Go Away

When enlightened darkness
is erased, I stumble blindly
through sun light. I am
a salamander feeling
my way unaccustomed,
wandering through dry land,
wondering about dry bones
scattered on ground too hard
to be my home–knowing
death welcomes us all
and drama can occur
any place, at any time.

Thunderstorm

Nothing but leftover gas
tells us something
beyond our control
has happened.

No radar, no instrument
we have devised
can explain origins,
source or outcomes.

Thunder comforts me.
I find satisfaction
in the heaven-sent reminder
that control is illusionary.

I am watching jays
and chickadees feeding
in gentle rain, apparently
unperturbed by thunder

echoing through oak-filled
hills, over the meadow
grass surrendered
to November frost.

What is the power of a word?
Storm is a misnomer—
at least today when sound
and fury feels good

like an awkward uncle
or a crusty friend hugging
you just a bit rougher
than expected.

The Art of Taking

for Chloe

Receive me
as you receive yourself.

Giving is a mirrored act.
The gift-giver first
gifts herself

with dignity, with trust
and the courage
the unknown demands.

Reach out
with both hands
and accept
what is meant for you.

Take it all in—
hold tight forever
all that love and life require

this exchange, this understanding
between hope and fear.

You gift me by taking—
just say *Thank You*—
and all will be well.

When Hawks Soar

for Gary Worth Moody

When hawks soar
in Santa Fe sky,
the world feels right.

Swift, merciful violence
balanced by beauty,
above austere, art-inspiring
landscape painting life
with purpose.

When first reporting
his terminal illness,
my friend told me
he would face it
with the sagacity
learned from a man
in Siberia: *Only
an American
would be arrogant
enough to believe his life
is worth more than
a good cigarette.*

I replied: *You're more
than that. You are
at least worth
a premium cigar.*

Hawks are nesting now
but soon they'll wing
their way through endless
cobalt sky, drifting
on updrafts with
magnificent majesty

before plummeting
onto prey—a terrifying
bolt of lightning
too pure, too brilliant
to be forgotten.

Ceremony of Release

with Gary Worth Moody

Miles off the main road, we enter wilderness.
We gather at a favorite spot of our friend—
the falconer—some remote peak overlooking
The Santa Fe River—rocky outcroppings,
juniper, cholla and prickly pear scattered
on descent deep into the canyon.

We have come to say goodbye to the man
who kept hawks, hunted with hawks
and wrote poems about hawks. The man
who loved and lived Caja del Rio.
We are welcomed into his wild sanctuary.

The *Ceremony of Release* is beginning.
Our Indigenous leaders, our intermediaries
in traditional dress, with drum and shaker,
with chanted prayers to the four directions,
and up to the sun, and kneeling to touch
earth—all this will prepare us, sanctify us,
so we may scatter his ashes to the winds,
sending him to his next reality.

We have all been cleansed with ritual smoke.
We have made our circular rotation, counter-
clockwise. We are listing as the shaman leads
us into this rite of passage

                    When I hear
the unmistakable soft shrill of a Red-Tailed
Hawk. I look up, and there he is—floating
above us, close enough that we can clearly
distinguish markings of his feathers, the head,
the face, the beak, features of color.

This magnificent sky angel circles four times
above us making intermittent calls.

We are all thinking the same thing–a couple
of us voice it: *It's Gary!*–we are looking,
pointing skyward, receiving the presence
of this hawk. Even the intercessor pauses
her prayers–captivated by this visitation.
After a few indescribable, holy moments,
the hawk rises on thermal currents, drifts
slowly out of sight–rising and disappearing.

We hold onto the view until there is nothing
but endless sky beyond us.

Then in the glowing haze of wonderment,
we lower our heads, return to prayer
before we will take our turn scattering ashes
over the ledge into timeless wind.

Rachmaninoff under the Stars

Hear swelling strings, accented
with riveting piano keys,
and the timpani too.

I sit stone-still—
my head tilted back, eyes
transfixed on nothing

when a large, dark bird,
an owl I guess,
floats silent, surreal

through my sight—
and I am reminded that darkness
has its own vision

of things unforeseeable.
I listen and I feel
and I believe

in the truth of everything,
even lies
which have a truth of their own.

When I Hear Cottonwood Leaves

On a sunny morning
in late October,
rippling–I imagine
an eternal river spilling
into me–water
I enjoy for now–but
will have to cross
some blue day.

On a sunny morning
in late October,
applauding the brilliance
shaping us–
a kinship unspoken,
scarcely known–
I'm happy just to be
related.

On a sunny morning
in late October,
singing yellow leaves–
a bunch of chickadees,
two crows, and a
yellow-rumped warbler.
A doe snorts–I am
what I hear.

Inspiration

When even Emily fails to inspire,
Bukowski seems polished.
The absence of art paralyzes—
how lost we become—endless
ocean waves promise nothing—
thriving is a hapless dream—
survival depends on so much
so far away. You settle
for Frost's *Snowy Evening,*
even *Desert Places*—at least
there you might stand, feel
Earth tapping your footfall,
trusting mirages to keep you
moving, if not believing.

Anonymity

Morning stretches burly arms,
holds like a tree.

Your heart feels the upward pull.
Everything rises. Light surrounds you

while you wait for release,
the moment the sky disappears

and you fold into the hours that claim
us, a thoughtless fish in a school

of habit, of custom, of dumb obedience—
the way light comes and goes

the way love and loss move
through a soundless universe

far deeper than any imagined sea—
burning dross forever falling

in darkness, into daylight—blurred
and ultimately nameless.

Like a Child, Believes All Things are Possible

Unmoved

Ruthless wind whips
the prairie–old grass
and red cedar angled,
groveling, unable
to stand upright.

A windmill, unmoved,
like an oil derrick–its
remaining blade
bent–others fallen
to the ground.

Sometimes a poem
writes itself, but choose
your metaphors
like politicians–with fear
and trembling.

Portrait in January

The cold Canadian River
clings to lifeless sand
beneath gray sky
driven by Siberian wind.

In this crucible of tyranny
created by baseless claims,
adored by sloppy imagination,
a black horse stands alone
at a wire, looking

at something, somewhere.
Such nobility, seemingly,
out of place.

Absence of Green

Tears well up
        in the chest,
        the heart we call it

and you feel it–
        the pressure
        when you slow down

and thoughts come on
        like sunrise
        or sunset

the moving sky
        never stopping–
        only you can pause

the motion called time,
        and feel tears
        that refuse to flow

but an unexplainable sadness,
        a short dispensation
        that conjures

a feeling for which no word
        exists–maybe
        sadness

maybe soft fear, or pacified
        rage or just
        uncertainty.

It is then you long
        for a friend
        to touch

you—an arm, or a hug
        across the shoulders,
        a quick cheek-kiss

to tell you that in your aloneness
        you are not
        alone

that sadness is not final
        that hope
        is just a leaf falling

through Autumn wind,
        yellow for now,
        an absence

of green leaves you empty,
        but memories of April
        also flutter

in the occasioned mind,
        and you draw breath
        for tomorrow.

False Spring

Anticipation gets the best of us.
Every year we feel the first fine sun
of February, and we find a false glow rising
around us, something stirring our slumber.
We move more. We feel energy we
had forgotten. We say things more loudly.
We're even giddy, at times.

Today the sun glistens
on Central Avenue in Hot Springs.
Magnolia shadows mark the sidewalk.
I hear a Cardinal between bubbling
water and revving motors.
The hardwoods are bare.
I think about red berries in holly
along the wall, as if a prick from these
green leaves might be a sign of sorts.

Do you believe in signs?
I can't say for sure for myself.
I observe signs. I think I interpret
signs. I fear signs. I guess
I'd have to say I don't trust signs.
So yes, my distrust means I believe.

The Stars and Stripes stand tall
above a National Park building.
This is not a trump-manipulated,
misguided patriotism—false
allegiance to a false god.
This flag has been posted long before
America turned Nazi. That flag,
in its ironic status of blessing us all,
becomes another mark of falsehood.
What it stands for, now, is only half
true. The blood of citizens recoils
at the divisive thought.

Shadows reshape as the sun climbs
higher, warms me, despite morning breeze.
A wintered Oak leaf flutters close by.
Its broken brown body signifies its past
green life, now long gone.
Its death-stage tells me what it is not–
tells me what it once was.

Can I trust new green will take its place?
Not now, not in February.
Now, the truth is not possible.
Now, only a promise of return–maybe–
if you have faith to believe–if you can trust
the life-giving flow of splashing water
soothing my anxious mind.

Every year Anticipation gets to us.
Blue February seems destined for a short life.
With an eager hop in our steps,
and a rise in our voice, we tell each other
how nice the day is–as if it's hard to believe
the sun has returned, that spring will return.
We say it aloud to each other.
Even strangers voice it. It's a bipartisan
chorus in our American tragedy–the sun
shines on the just and the unjust alike,
warms the sleeveless arms of the bigot
and the one trying to live The Beatitudes–
but is it a false sensation?

To be gracious in a time of hate
is today's challenge. Discipleship has never
been easy. The memory of springs past,
and the fear of summer approaching–
encroaching with its promised sweltering
injustice–provides a moment of stasis.
But we can't remain here.
This emotional space cannot last.

One week ago, the temperature was in single
digits all day long. Maybe the nadir
has passed–but the shadows of winter,

the signs of frigid, fucked-up humanity
are with us.

                    I'm not sure we can escape.

If I'm a lifeless, broken, colorless leaf
wind-blown into an alley–destined
to decompose, alone, displaced,
out of sight–not even salvageable
for compost–in that deterioration,
I remember the green I once knew–
the green that I was.

The Slow, Endless Journey

for Kai Coggin & my students
Hot Springs National Park

We think of life accelerating–
too fast for comfort–soon death
is upon us–and even thoughts
of the next life (in various forms
& manifestations), however we
imagine eternity–speeds past
us in our hard-driven bodies,
through avalanching minds–
this bodily existence,
this emotional threshold
also seems to be rushed–
the speed of sound seems normal.

But sitting beside a pool
of springing hot water, purling
from the core of Earth,
I am reminded that it takes
four thousand years for rain
to make its fallen way
to Earth, to seep through cracks
and crevices, dripping, moving
more than three thousand miles
to the center of our planet–

Four Thousand Years!

and then another four hundred
years for that same water
to be thrust upward
to the surface, to reappear
in this pool I now see and hear.

I think of each drop
of rainwater as a soul
embodied in human experience–

and each, a little, individual,
isolated hero–descending
into the core
of sun-like heat,
then rising upward, upward,
upward to be splashed
so beautifully transparent
on the surface, once again.

The Hero's Journey takes 4400 years!

Water before me was rain
over four thousand years ago!

Tomorrow's rain
will disappear beneath the Earth
only to reappear an eon
or two from now.
But it will reappear.
It will resurface.

What falls below,
what is driven underground
will not cease to be–

It will only intensify,
become too hot to believe.
and will surely rise again
for some distant, lucky observer
I can only imagine.

I think about that couple
standing by the steaming pool–
their in-love loveliness
so evident as they embrace
to take a selfie–they
are temporary–do they know
they are also endless?

I hope their love remains.
Maybe it will. Maybe it will not.

But Love remains—that absolute
category will fill some destined heart.

Brown leaves are falling
from November's trees.
Autumn sun brightens the path
of tourists—each person
stops at this pool—every traveler
has a moment of reflection.
They can't help touching
the steaming hot water.
I watch them predictably shake
the dripping heat
from their fingers

Unaware they are rehearsing
for a time when their bodies
will return to dust, will decompose
and become flushed
in the tidal force of rainwater,
pushing them down, down,
down
          ever so slowly,
so magnificently righteous
to the center of our planet.

They are touching family.

Symphony with the Letter M

Mahler's melancholy melody moves me
past morbidity–his mood in music
makes me marvel at his mimesis,
his movements meandering, menacing
the mundane–his intimations reminding
me simultaneously of mortality
and immortality, mollifying my mercurial
soul mixing pathos with memory–
meticulously improvising, mitigating
the malicious malaise that mocks humanity,
before moving upward, outward, beyond
the muddied mirror of existence
marred by merit unclaimed–a monstrous
moroseness, meddling with my mind's
misperceiving, past mere metaphor,
for myopic misgivings marked by
man-made misery–mutating, emerging,
confirming moments to mold me
in mystery–making a new man on
a new mountain with a new mythology,
imminent if misunderstood–maintaining
the soul until miracles seem normal,
if only manifest in the mind attempting
to meld with matter's molecules
of miscalculations, misinformation
wrought with intimidating malevolence–
even if manipulated, ever in motion.

Between Tulsa and Forever

Light. And a lady
much too young.
Even the word *friend* seems distant

but here we are—
retracing where we've been,
speaking the same words

despite differences—
do we mean the same thing?
Ice cream! (Diabetes be damned.)

Full, fresh and fun—
but frozen in time
like the man sleeping in the cradle

of a church wall—
the street mostly quiet now—
a one-way street we entered

going the wrong direction—
the taste of butterscotch
mixing with midnight chocolate.

Light. Here we are.
Here we are some place remembered
between Tulsa and forever

where downtown sky falls
between peaks of buildings
too tall, too gray—

and for all their intimidation—
too timid to be of much use
to one trying to hold light

in one hand
while swishing shadows away
with the other.

Beyond

Wind and leafless Pecan trees
in late March.

A deeply insecure person
on my mind.
Fear and poetry
and projected self-loathing
and an un-groomed rose bush
that flowers pink
every year, despite neglect.

Two grandsons.
Uncertain plumbing
and the threat of prairie fire,
wind-blown
like an ancient script
when Nomads simply picked up
and moved

beyond danger, beyond

false hopes of permanence
and family followed
the herd
and God was in the stars
and the soil spoke
and you listened—
everything listened

and rivers rose and fell
like sunlight
and poems were chanted.

Wind and leafless Pecan trees
in late March

and surviving kept us sane.

Double Rainbow–Just East of Wanette

We need all the help we can get
out here in this confusing place
where virtue can be abstract
and prosperity is a dream
lost on tattered sleeves of hope.

Light rain, at first, then harder,
will soon erase the sun-lit prism.
Colors intensify into focus
for a few glimmering moments

and then this precocious morning
will become like so many others.
But I did catch that double ring
of colors, and felt almost happy

the way a shy child receives
a Christmas gift wrapped in bows
except I know what the child
does not yet understand–
how days add up
and colors come and go.

Acorns Remembered in May

Honking geese. Chipping birds.
The first band of sunlight
trimming the treetops. A moth
seems lost in hapless flight.
Heavy dew. Hidden flowers.
William Stafford somewhere
in the background. Jane
Kenyon and James Wright
are never far away.

To see it all end this way
while thinking of options,
other histories you have believed
now falling, too frequently,
so silently, that any voice
raised in protest sounds like noise.
Dissent is treated as disease.

But the soil beneath the oaks
absorbs the dying
with passive certainty,
and decomposition,
somehow, is necessary
and always new.

Lamentation

It's pretty easy to be a prophet
in Oklahoma–a place overrun
with social ills disregarded
by the privileged few, disguised
behind masks worn thin
in arrogant, willful ignorance–
posing as holy tough guys–
as if God needs their validation,
as if Christ is a badass who recruits
boys to become obedient champions,
signing up for passive-aggressive
duty–knife blades regressing
to stone, deliberately dull,
wielded with delightful delusion.

Gray Dawn Cedar

A sister in central Texas
listens for birds
on her front porch. Coffee
and sunrise and quiet

and here jonquils
beaten by midnight hail
are bent

wounded, recoiled.
Their color
dulled, bruised

beneath a gray dawn
cedar that poses
over land

riddled, but
reclaiming. From here
to Texas and back
wind coils

and rattles, but
we have learned to survive
intrusion

and even in days
without color,
we find a pattern

and we listen close
for a new breeze
coming soon

that carries the breath
of chickadees and
mockingbirds across a river
gorged with grief.

Illusions

Clinging like sweat in July,
false faces of reality
confuse those who don't look
closely enough.

Look again past dead limbs,
through green oaks,
up to pale blue sky
holding wrens and crows.

Look even higher
and follow the kite,
and later the nighthawk.
Follow them all,

feel their freedom,
escape these lower realms,
these deceptive depths.
Invention is a lullaby

mothers sing, a memory
to which old men cling
like smoke from fire
no longer burning.

In the Darkness of Dawn

Stretched and measured,
you don't know what you have left
to give, let alone to keep clear
yourself, if not solvent.

Oppressive heat dulls everything.
Turned like sausage on a grill,
the thing to do is walk upright,
but the back bends
and the mind overcorrects.

Finally, in blue-black-pitched hues
of New Mexico sky, temperature falls,
and like a rodent, you scurry
before light for something to eat
and for water–*Dios Mio*–
always for water!

You remember the scarlet blaze
on the table-rock above the river,
the falcon in flight, bringing
food to nest where hunger cries
split the morning air.

Smoke from a distant fire
filtered through sunbeams
like arrows shot between ledges,
and you know time is short.

Torn between pursuing pleasure
and responding to pain
so fierce among us–throughout
our world–so common,
so commandeering

you doubt a change of season
will relieve the suffering.
So you suffer by proxy,

and your pleasure is compromised—
sometimes to the point of envy
for the dead, remembered
only by occasional, short-lived
ceremony.

In the darkness of dawn
you remember a time when you
were knocked off your stride.
You were the devil's piñata.
In their sadistic circle,
laughing demons beat you
just for the hell of it.

A man caught unaware,
your only glimmer of hope
was to land on your knees—
but how to walk and crawl
when both seem necessary

how to receive grace
and to return fire
when both seem natural

when the comfort of dawn fades,
and white-hot sun blinds
and bleaches everything?

Even My Running

Death has the power to hold us
By the most subtle ties.
                    —Baudelaire

Will you join me
in bondage
invisible but sure?

Even my running
only goes as long
as the leash.

I must tell myself
the truth
that never will die:

Everything new
is as old
as the Earth.

My little joys,
my misperceived
fate

untethered
only in dreams
will not let me go.

Heaven and Hell
and everything
between

shapes the soul—
that self-adoring mask
I wear

endures
but for a season,
contends with pride.

Like leaves on a tree,
even water
moving downstream

to the sea,
to the clouds–
this frail eternity

rains life down
on us
where death abides.

The body craves health,
the mind, sanity,
but wind forever blows.

Withering

Learn first to wither!
          —Conrad Aiken

The Garden is no place for a pilgrim.
Snakes and sinners cannot abide bliss.
Exile is the call I answer–and I answer
with conflicted pride–knowing
what I know now, knowing trouble
starts at home, starts within.

How much effort I have spent toiling,
trying to grow, prosper, flourish–
with so little preparation for death,
how to return to dust.

To bloom may be natural,
but withering must be learned.

Don't label me morbid.
Mark me, rather, as one living
among the weeds–one
whose brief Garden tenure
taught him something basic–
maybe even scared him
to the point of abeyance.

Remember, expulsion did not
put an end to growth;
it only made cultivation an art.

I am pruning myself
to fit the patterned rows
I have plowed and I have planted
under a vagrant sun

that worrisome life
bearing so much, yet
always bending toward home.

Enough

The stars speak to me:

Give, give—
give yourself
to something
that cannot last,
something that burned out
before you even knew yourself

Who you are,
what you thought you might be
with your delusions
of grandeur

          popping all around
every decade or so—
essentially blowing hot gas—

and from one perspective, that's true,
but from another view,
how the fire falls on starry nights
speaking to anyone who has courage
enough to lift his eyes
and see.

Give, give—
give yourself the stars say to me.

Their voice must be seen
to be heard,
must be believed to be here—
Now—with us all.

Give the stars speak to me.
Give yourself
to something
that cannot last,

Who you are
is not what you were.

All you know–Now–
is what you see, Now.

Fire falling–Now,
that energy filling space Now–
making us

       un-lonely,
       un-suspected,
       un-unappreciated

undoing a darkness.

Forget eternity.

It is Now that is seen
and you see what you give.

Speak stars, speak to me.
Never go silent.
Never take me back
to that void un-seeable.

Let's fall together
by giving.

All that I am I see
and that is enough
for Now.

Turning Gray

So I burn
until one day I look
in the mirror
and am grateful for the ash
in my face. Heart
smolders, and I know
gray is the blessing

named survival, know
the great journey
will one day end, and
will see the seasons
of my life have fallen
into place. If I knew then,
well, how judicious

I might have been,
but honestly, probably
would have made
the same mistakes because
who can know the future
when the present
is a ball of fire?

Like a Child

He closes the curtains
on the east windows
to save a degree or two

puts Schubert on stereo,
sits in a shaded room,
time-travels to Austria

with the miracle of technology,
is soothed by genius,
by something past

reclaiming his beating heart,
his soul in tune
with the eternal

pleasure makes possible,
reinforcing the need
of blessing composed

in *Ave Maria*, augmented
by Romantic poets, admired
even by Beethoven.

Quietly, alone, he listens
and like a child, believes
all things are possible.

Acknowledgments

Grateful acknowledgment is made to the editors where the following poems first appeared:

"Between Tulsa and Forever": *Literature Today: An International Literary Journal*
"Double Rainbow–Just East of Wanette": *Orchards Poetry Journal*
"Like a Breeze in Gray Dawn": *Deep South Magazine*
"Minnesota Reign": *Broad Daylight: An Outcrying of Poetry in Tribute to Renee Nicole Good*
"Rachmaninoff under the Stars": *Notes of Light & Dark: Southwestern Aubades & Nocturnes*
"Symphony with the Letter M": *Windward Review*
"The Art of Taking": *eMerge Magazine*
"The Music I Hear": *Behind the Rain vol.15*
"Withering": *San Pedro River Review*

About the Author

Ken Hada lives in the rural Crosstimbers of central Oklahoma where his close relationship to the land inspires much of his writing. A literary ecologist, Ken's work blends the challenges of modern society, the questions of spirituality, identity, culture and mortality with the rhythms of nature–what he calls "The Natural Self." Information about his work may be found at kenhada.org.